Charlotte
Bacon

Good Dogs, Great Listeners

The Story of Charlotte, Lily and the Litter

by Renata Bowers
with JoAnn and Joel Bacon

pictures by Michael Chesworth

Charlotte's Litter, Inc.

Sandy Hook • Connecticut

For Charlotte
Forever and Always Loved
May your life encourage others to Be Bold

First edition.

Library of Congress Control Number: 2014959329

ISBN Hardcover: 978-0-9863001-1-0
ISBN Special First Edition: 978-0-9863001-0-3

Printed in Minnesota, USA.

Renata Bowers and Michael Chesworth also are writer and illustrator, respectively,
of the Frieda B. series of children's books. To learn more, visit www.FriedaB.com.

Charlotte's Litter, Inc. is a supporter of Newtown Kindness and its programs.

Lily is a dog with ears soft as velvet, fur the color of caramel and cream, eyes like cocoa, and a heart that belongs to Charlotte.

Charlotte is a girl with wavy brown hair, silver-blue eyes, dimples on either side of her chin, a bold sense of adventure, and a deep love for dogs.

Especially Lily.

Meet Charlotte's Litter. A collection of stuffed dogs who, along with Lily, are Charlotte's most constant companions.

Fetch

Big Henrey

Little Henrey

Special

Chocolate

Lollipop

Charlotte and Lily and the whole Litter love, love, love to read, to get lost in the pages of a book, and allow the story to take them to new worlds and adventures.

But this wasn't always so…

Not all that long ago, Charlotte believed without a smidgen of doubt that reading was just plain boring. When told to read a book, she'd loudly proclaim, "Who can *read*, when there's so much fun stuff to *do?*"

It was summer. Charlotte was supposed to read a book a day. Her parents reminded her that if she wanted to be a veterinarian, she needed to be a good reader.

Charlotte did want to be a veterinarian.

Very much.

But she didn't want to read.

Not at all.

So, often she did something else instead.

One day, there was a book to read about a great ocean voyage. Charlotte did not want to read it. She yawned wide and said to her dogs, "Let's go get a drink of water."

"Good Dogs!" she said as Lily and The Litter faithfully followed her to the bathroom sink, where she turned on the water.

While looking for a cup, Charlotte spotted a toy boat on the counter.

And a pink plastic fish.

And a seashell.

And while she showed the boat and fish and shell to her dogs, the sink overflowed onto the floor.

So there was an ocean.

And Charlotte became a captain, and her dogs the crew.

And it suddenly was a great voyage,

and all very exciting.

Until...

...the ocean seeped under the door and into the hallway.

"CHARLOTTE!" her father cried, "What's happening in there?"

"Dad," said Charlotte, "can't you see? I'm a captain and we're on the great ocean!"

"But you've made a great mess, and you're supposed to be reading," her dad scolded. "Charlotte, you're not being a good listener."

Another day, there was a book to read about a princess and a castle and a grand ball. Charlotte did not want to read it.

She yawned wide and said to her dogs, "Let's go get a blanket."

"Good Dogs!" she said as Lily and The Litter faithfully followed her into her mom's closet, where she reached for a blanket.

While reaching, Charlotte spotted a shiny pink dress.

And pink shoes.

And a scarf.

And while she showed the dress and shoes and scarf to her dogs,
she caught sight of her mom's makeup.

So the room became a castle.

And Charlotte became the princess and her dogs the guests.

And it suddenly was a grand ball,

and all very exciting.

Until…

…her mom spotted a trail of makeup leading into her bedroom.

"CHARLOTTE!" her mother cried, "What's happening in there?"

"Mom," said Charlotte, "can't you see? I'm a princess and we're at a grand ball!"

"But you've made a grand mess, and you're supposed to be reading," her mom scolded. "Charlotte, you're not being a good listener."

On yet another day, there was a book to read about a boy who had just earned his black belt. Charlotte did not want to read it.

She yawned wide and said to her dogs, "Let's go get a fluffier pillow."

"Good Dogs!" she said as Lily and The Litter faithfully followed her to the living room, where she scooped up her favorite pillow.

While scooping, Charlotte noticed there were lots of throw pillows.

And sofa cushions.

And a bean bag.

And then, she thought about just how many pillows there were all over the house. She scooped up every last one and brought them all to her room.

So her room became a Tae Kwon Do studio.

And Charlotte became the master and her dogs the students.

And it suddenly was a romping good time

with lots of kicking and punching and stretching.

Until…

…poor Lily

fell off the bed

and hurt her leg.

"MOM! DAD!" Charlotte cried,

"Come quick! Lily's hurt!!"

Charlotte and her mom and dad and brother quickly and gently got Lily into the car and drove to the veterinarian. Usually, Charlotte loved to go there, to dream about what it would be like to be an animal doctor herself one day.

But not today.

Today she was too worried about Lily.

Charlotte tried to be brave for herself and for Lily as the doctor examined Lily's leg. It was hard to be brave.

At last, the doctor looked up and said, "Charlotte, Lily is going to be okay, but she's going to need lots of rest. No running or jumping or playing. You'll need to find quiet ways to love her and to keep her company. Can you think of any good ways to do that?"

Charlotte looked at Lily, then looked up at her parents.

And then, she knew.

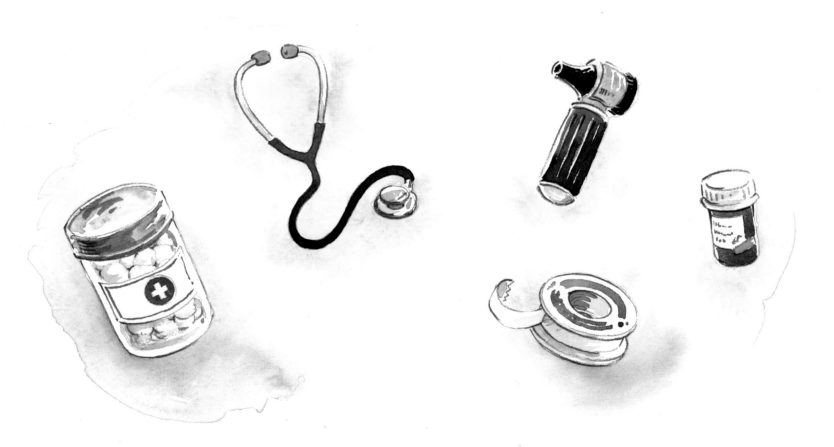

"I could read to her," she said. "I have lots of books."

"That," said the doctor, "is an excellent idea."

And that is just how Charlotte and Lily and The Litter came to love, love, love to read books. Especially books about animals, and veterinarians.

With time, Lily's leg healed, and she and Charlotte and The Litter were back to running and jumping and playing.

But they never again passed up the opportunity to read a good book, together.

Good dogs.

Great listeners.

Good night.